M000191751

A PURE HEART

The Window to God

Charles & Anne Hummel

ZondervanPublishingHouse

Grand Rapids, Michigan

A Division of HarperCollinsPublishers

Requests for information should be addressed to:
Zondervan Publishing House
Grand Rapids, MI 49530

ISBN 0-310-59643-2

Edited by Jack Kuhatschek
Cover design by John M. Lucas
Cover photograph by Mike Carter
Interior design by Louise Bauer

Printed in the United States of America

93   94   95 . 96   97   98 / ❖ DP / 10   9   8   7   6   5   4   3   2   1

Contents

The Beatitude Series

Welcome to the Beatitude Series. This series is designed to help you develop the eight character qualities found in those whom Jesus calls "blessed."

The Beatitudes are among the best-known and best-loved words of Jesus. They form the heart of the Sermon on the Mount, found in Matthew 5–7 and Luke 6:17–49. In eight brief statements Jesus describes the lifestyle that God desires and rewards:

> *Blessed are the poor in spirit,*
>   *for theirs is the kingdom of heaven.*
> *Blessed are those who mourn,*
>   *for they will be comforted.*
> *Blessed are the meek,*
>   *for they will inherit the earth.*
> *Blessed are those who hunger and thirst for righteousness,*
>   *for they will be filled.*
> *Blessed are the merciful,*
>   *for they will be shown mercy.*
> *Blessed are the pure in heart,*
>   *for they will see God.*

Blessed are the peacemakers,
  for they will be called sons of God.
Blessed are those who are persecuted because of righteousness,
  for theirs is the kingdom of heaven.

The Beatitudes turn the world's values upside down. We are tempted to say: "*Wretched* are the poor, for they have so little money. *Wretched* are those who mourn, for no one will hear their cries. *Wretched* are the meek, for they will be trampled by the powerful." Yet Jesus shatters our stereotypes and asserts that the poor will be rich, the mourners will be comforted, and the meek will inherit everything. What a strange kingdom he offers!

In recent years there has been some confusion about the kind of blessing Christ promises in these verses. The Beatitudes have been described as "God's prescription for happiness." One book has even called them "The Be-Happy Attitudes."

The Greek word *makarios* can mean "happy." J. B. Phillips translates the opening words of each beatitude, "How happy are . . . !" Nevertheless, John Stott writes:

> It is seriously misleading to render *makarios* "happy." For happiness is a subjective state, whereas Jesus is making an objective judgment about these people. He is declaring not what they may feel like ("happy"), but what God thinks of them and what on that account they are: they are "blessed."[1]

The eight guides in the Beatitude Series give you an in-depth look at each beatitude. But Jesus is not describing eight different types of people—some who are meek, others who are merciful, and still others who are peacemakers. He desires to see all eight character qualities in every one of his followers.

That's a tall order! Only those who enter Christ's kingdom by faith can expect such a transformation. And only those who serve the King can enjoy his rewards.

Our prayer is that The Beatitude Series will give you a clearer and deeper grasp of what it truly means to be blessed.

HOW TO USE THE BEATITUDE SERIES

The Beatitude Series is designed to be flexible. You can use the guides in any order that is best for you or your group. They are ideal for Sunday-school classes, small groups, one-on-one relationships, or as materials for your quiet times.

Because each guide contains only six studies, you can easily explore more than one beatitude. In a Sunday-school class, any two guides can be combined for a quarter (twelve weeks), or the entire series can be covered in a year.

Each study deliberately focuses on a limited number of passages, usually only one or two. That allows you to see each passage in its context, avoiding the temptation of prooftexting and the frustration of "Bible hopscotch" (jumping from verse to verse). If you would like to look up additional passages, a Bible concordance will give the most help.

The Beatitude Series helps you *discover* what the Bible says rather than simply *telling* you the answers. The questions encourage you to think and to explore options rather than merely to fill in the blanks with one-word answers.

Leader's notes are provided in the back of each guide. They show how to lead a group discussion, provide additional information on questions, and suggest ways to deal with problems that may come up in the discussion. With such helps, someone with little or no experience can lead an effective study.

SUGGESTIONS FOR INDIVIDUAL STUDY

1. Begin each study with prayer. Ask God to help you understand the passage and to apply it to your life.

2. A good modern translation, such as the *New International Version,* the *New American Standard Bible,* or the *New Revised Standard Version,* will give you the most help. Questions in this guide, however, are based on the *New International Version.*

3. Read and reread the passage(s). You must know what the passage says before you can understand what it means and how it applies to you.

4. Write your answers in the space provided in the study guide. This will help you to clearly express your understanding of the passage.

5. Keep a Bible dictionary handy. Use it to look up any unfamiliar words, names, or places.

SUGGESTIONS FOR GROUP STUDY

1. Come to the study prepared. Careful preparation will greatly enrich your time in group discussion.

2. Be willing to join in the discussion. The leader of the group will not be lecturing but will encourage people to discuss what they have learned in the passage. Plan to share what God has taught you in your individual study.

3. Stick to the passage being studied. Base your answers on the verses being discussed rather than on outside authorities such as commentaries or your favorite author or speaker.

4. Try to be sensitive to the other members of the group. Listen attentively when they speak, and be affirming whenever you can. This will encourage more hesitant members of the group to participate.

5. Be careful not to dominate the discussion. By all means participate! But allow others to have equal time.

6. If you are the discussion leader, you will find additional suggestions and helpful ideas in the leader's notes at the back of the guide.

Note

1. *The Message of the Sermon on the Mount* (Downers Grove, Ill.: InterVarsity Press, 1978), p. 33.

Introducing
A Pure Heart

Blessed are the pure in heart,
for they will see God.

According to Jewish tradition, when the high priest entered the most sacred part of the temple on the Day of Atonement—a room he alone was allowed to enter—the other priests tied a rope to his ankle. That way, if he was struck dead in God's presence, they could safely pull him out!

When Moses asked to see God's glory, the Lord replied, "You cannot see my face, for no one may see me and live" (Ex. 33:20). The apostle Paul describes God as the One "who lives in unapproachable light, whom no one has seen or can see" (1 Tim. 6:16). And the apostle John confirms the fact that "no one has ever seen God" (John 1:18; 1 John 4:12).

The problem, of course, is our sin. Just as people are vaporized in the million-degree heat of a nuclear blast, so we cannot withstand the intense presence of a holy God.

Yet Jesus promises that the day will come when the impossible will be possible, when we will see what no one has or can now see. In the beatitudes he makes the startling claim, "Blessed are the pure in heart, for they will see God."

Seeing the Father—and truly knowing him—is the ultimate hope of every Christian. Christ assures us that our hope will not be disappointed. "The pure in heart will see God—now with the eyes of faith and finally in the dazzling brilliance of the beatific vision."[1]

Christ's promise also implies that moral purity is possible for those who follow him. If only the "pure in heart" will see God, then such purity must be within the reach of his disciples. But what does it mean to be pure in heart? And how can sinful people like us ever hope to achieve that purity?

This study guide can help you answer these questions. The first study begins with Jesus' explanation of what it means to be "pure in heart" in terms of our thoughts and actions, our inner motivation, and our outward practice. The second study looks at David's experience of confession and restoration. Studies three and four consider instructions for holy living in the letters of the apostles Peter and John. The final two studies help us prepare to see God both now and in the ultimate vision of the new heaven and earth.

May this study challenge and encourage you to have a pure heart so that you can see God in a new and fresh way.

Charles & Anne Hummel

Note

1. D. A. Carson, *Matthew,* The Expositor's Bible Commentary (Grand Rapids, Mich.: Zondervan, 1984), p. 135.

Purifying Our Thoughts

MATTHEW 5:21–22, 27–30; 23:23–32

A well-known proverb states: "The thought is father of the deed." Our thoughts often influence our actions more than we realize. Although actions may speak louder than words, behind them both lie our attitudes.

Soon after he gave the Beatitudes, Jesus addressed this issue with a startling application that challenged traditional teaching about murder and adultery.

1. How do your thoughts influence some of the ways you act?

2. Read Matthew 5:21–22, 27–30. How are murder and anger related (vv. 21–22)?

3. What does your anger, sarcasm, or insult do to another person?

What does it do to you?

4. According to Jesus, what is the full meaning of the commandment regarding adultery (vv. 27–28)?

5. What can we do to avoid lustful thoughts or to deal with them when they occur?

6. How does Jesus intend us to understand his graphic warnings in verses 29–30?

7. In what situations might you need to "gouge out an eye" or "cut off a hand" to avoid sinning?

What realistic actions would such temptations call for?

8. How do Jesus' statements about murder and adultery challenge us to go deeper than the superficial righteousness of the Pharisees (see v. 20)?

9. Read Matthew 23:23–32. What images does Jesus use to describe the Pharisees' attitudes and actions?

What kinds of hypocrisy do they portray?

10. What examples of hypocrisy do you see in your church? in yourself?

11. In what ways were the religious leaders deceiving themselves (vv. 29–32)?

How can we avoid falling into the same trap?

MEMORY VERSE

Do not think that I have come to abolish the Law or the Prophets; I have not come to abolish them but to fulfill them.

Matthew 5:17

BETWEEN STUDIES

For a better understanding of what really makes us unclean, read Jesus' discussion with the Pharisees in Mark 7:14–23. Classify in the list which items are thoughts, attitudes, words, and actions. As you ponder these sins, ask God to show you which, if any, in your own life call for repentance and forgiveness.

2

Whiter Than Snow

PSALM 51

King David, righteous ruler and prolific psalmist, was called a man after God's own heart (1 Sam. 13:14). Yet through a combination of lust, deceit, and intrigue he committed adultery with Bathsheba and planned the death of her husband Uriah.

When the prophet Nathan confronted David with his sin and its consequences, the king confessed, "I have sinned against the Lord." Nathan then replied, "The Lord has taken away your sin. You are not going to die" (2 Sam. 12:13).

In Psalm 51 David confesses his sin and asks the Lord to recreate within him the pure heart required to enter God's presence. David's prayer can be an effective model for our sin and restoration.

1. Why do people find it hard to confess their sins and ask for forgiveness?

2. Read Psalm 51. What synonyms does David use for sin in verses 1–6?

Explain what each one means.

3. What characteristics of God give David confidence for asking forgiveness?

4. How can David say that his acts of adultery and murder were sins only against God (v. 4)?

5. What does the fact that we are sinful from the time of our conception tell us about the nature and extent of sin (v. 5)?

6. What specific actions does David request of God in verses 1–9?

What does each action do for the sinner?

7. What new insight have you gained from these verses about the nature of sin and its consequences?

8. Express in your own words the heart of David's prayer in verse 10.

9. What does David request for himself in verses 10–12?

Why are these important to us in our daily lives?

10. What are the external social consequences of a renewed personal relationship with God (vv. 13–15, 18–19)?

11. Describe the kinds of sacrifices God does and does not desire from us (vv. 16–17).

What does it mean to have a "broken spirit" and a "broken and contrite heart" (v. 17)?

12. In what ways might you be offering God a "sacrifice" of Christian service as a substitute for a "broken and contrite heart"?

13. In a few minutes of silence, focus on one sin you want to confess. In your prayer select one word for the sin, one word for God's character to which you appeal, and one word for the action he takes in response.

MEMORY VERSE

> *Create in me a pure heart, O God,*
> *and renew a steadfast spirit within me.*

Psalm 51:10

BETWEEN STUDIES

For the details of David's sin and its consequences read 2 Samuel 11:1–12:14. In this narrative you will see the craftiness and deceit David used to cover his adultery. You will also see how the prophet Nathan carried out an assignment that might have cost his life. The narrative spells out the dire consequences of David's sinful conduct for himself and his family.

Also read the Ten Commandments in Exodus 20:1–17 and note that David broke the sixth, seventh, and tenth—half of those dealing with human relationships.

3

Walking in the Light

1 JOHN 1:1–2:11

In the Carlsbad Caverns of southeastern New Mexico, you descend hundreds of feet into the earth. Your journey takes you down winding corridors past dripping stalactites, clusters of stalagmites, and dark holes that drop into oblivion.

At one point the tour guide announces: "We would like you to experience the *total* absence of light." And with a flick of a switch, you are plunged into a black darkness that is complete and overwhelming. With momentary fear, you realize how lost and helpless and disoriented you are in that condition. But just before claustrophobia sets in, the switch is thrown, the lights come on, and you return to the surface. What a relief!

In 1 John 1:1–2:11 the apostle warns us about the dangers of walking in darkness and the joys of walking in the light.

1. What major temptations are thrust on us by our secular culture?

2. Read 1 John 1:1–10. What evidence does John give for the validity of his message (vv. 1–2)?

Why is this evidence so important?

3. Why is John writing this letter (vv. 3–4)?

How is our fellowship with God connected to our relationship with each other?

4. Anyone can claim to have fellowship with God (v. 6). But how is our conduct the ultimate test of our claim (vv. 6–7)?

5. What does it mean to "walk in the light" and to "walk in darkness" (see also John 8:12)?

How does walking in the light differ from sinlessness?

6. If a person claims to be without sin, what does that reveal about his spiritual condition (vv. 8, 10; see also John 8:31–37; 42–47)?

7. As we walk in the light and confess our sins, how does God deal with our sin (vv. 7, 9)?

8. How have you experienced God's provision for dealing with sin in your life (v. 9)?

9. Read 1 John 2:1–11. When we do sin, why is God willing and able to forgive our sin (vv. 1–2)?

10. According to John, how can we be sure that we know Christ, that we are not just making an empty claim (vv. 3–6)?

11. John focuses on a basic principle in verses 7–11. How can it be both old and new?

12. Why would love for our brother, rather than love for God, serve as a test for living in the light?

13. How has this passage helped you understand what it means—and doesn't mean—to "walk in the light"?

MEMORY VERSE

If we confess our sins, he is faithful and just and will forgive us our sins and purify us from all unrighteousness.

1 John 1:9

BETWEEN STUDIES

According to John, what we *claim* to believe or to experience must be validated by our *conduct*. Either way, our claims and conduct have certain spiritual *implications*. Using the chart below, write down some of the claims being made in 1 John1:5–2:11, the conduct being practiced, and the implications that follow.

Then write down some of the claims you make about your spiritual life and relationship with God. Does your conduct support or refute that claim? What, then, are the implications?

Claim	Conduct	Implication

For further teaching on love, how it is exemplified in the life and death of Jesus, and how it should be practically evidenced in our lives, meditate on 1 John 3:11–24.

4

A Holy Nation

1 PETER 1:13–2:10

It is not surprising that our morally permissive culture has largely dropped the word "holy" from its vocabulary. Except for the exclamation "holy smoke" and the sarcastic epithet "holy Joe" for a too-pious person, the word is rarely heard. Holy living grounded in the character of God has given way to a culturally acceptable norm: "If it feels good, do it."

In the moral wilderness of his own day, the apostle Peter urges Christians to fulfill their high calling as a "holy nation, a people belonging to God." In this study we will discover what that calling involves.

1. Where do the current moral standards of our country come from?

2. Read 1 Peter 1:13–25. Verse 13 begins Peter's call to action. In what three ways should we respond to the gift of salvation (v. 13)?

How would you explain the meaning of each command?

3. Peter warns us against being conformed to the evil desires of our past (v. 14). What evil desires are prevalent in our culture?

4. How does God's holiness motivate you to "be holy in all you do" (vv. 15–16)?

5. Practically speaking, how can we live as strangers in our own culture (v. 17)?

6. How should the high price of our salvation (vv. 18–21) keep us from returning to our former way of life?

7. Give some practical examples of how we can "love one another deeply, from the heart" (v. 22).

8. In verses 23–25, what kinds of "seeds" and plants are temporary and which are permanent?

9. Read 2:1–10. How would you explain each of the attitudes Peter urges us to get rid of (v. 1)?

10. How does Peter's illustration about newborn babies help you understand how we can grow as Christians (vv. 2–3)?

11. Peter compares us to "living stones" in verses 4–6. What does this comparison tell us about Jesus Christ and our relationship to him?

What are the different reactions to the "cornerstone" or "capstone" mentioned in verses 6–8?

12. In verse 9 what is the significance of each term Peter uses to describe the church?

13. In what ways can you "declare the praises of God" among your friends?

14. How does Peter describe our "before and after" story in verse 10?

15. How has salvation in Christ made a difference in your life and relationships?

MEMORY VERSES

But just as he who called you is holy, so be holy in all you do; for it is written: "Be holy, because I am holy."

1 Peter 1:15–16

BETWEEN STUDIES

Peter compares us to newborn babies, a holy priesthood, and a holy nation. Consider how you should respond in each of these roles:

- ❑ Like a newborn, take time to drink deeply of God's Word throughout the week.
- ❑ As a holy priest, what spiritual sacrifices can you offer to God today?
- ❑ As a citizen in God's holy nation, how might you serve or encourage another Christian this week?

5

Preparing to See God

PSALM 24

Suppose you were invited to the White House for a visit with the President of the United States. How would you prepare for the occasion? What would you feel as you walked down the hall toward the Oval Office? How would you react in the presence of the Commander-in-chief of America's armed forces?

In Psalm 24, King David pictures a ruler far greater than himself or any other head of state—the King of glory. Here we are told what it means to meet the Lord Almighty and how we must prepare for coming into his presence.

1. In what specific ways do you prepare yourself for worshiping God?

2. Read Psalm 24. This psalm is often divided into three sections: verses 1–2, 3–6, and 7–10. What brief title would you give to each section?

3. Why is the Lord worthy of our obedience and worship (vv. 1–2)?

4. "The hill of the LORD" (v. 3) was Mount Zion, site of the tabernacle and later temple. What central question does the psalmist ask, and how does he answer it?

5. Why are "clean hands and a pure heart" required for fellowship with God?

6. What kind of "blessing" and "vindication" do you think those with clean hands and a pure heart will receive (v. 5)?

7. Why do you think the two sins of idolatry and swearing falsely are singled out (v. 4)?

How prevalent in Israel might they have been at that time? Explain.

8. What does it mean to "seek" God or "seek [his] face" (v. 6)?

In what specific ways can we do this?

9. "Gates" and "ancient doors" (vv. 7, 9) probably refer to the gates of Jerusalem. How does David describe the God of Israel in verses 7–10?

What does each title reveal about the God we worship?

10. How does this description of God motivate you to approach him with "clean hands and a pure heart"?

11. Conclude with a brief time of silence in which you respond to God in a prayer inspired by this psalm.

MEMORY VERSES

> *Who may ascend the hill of the LORD?*
> *Who may stand in his holy place?*
> *He who has clean hands and a pure heart.*
>
> Psalm 24:3–4

BETWEEN STUDIES

Prepare yourself for worshiping God in the following ways:

- ❏ In what specific ways do you need to "clean your hands" and "purify your heart"?
- ❏ What idols do you need to renounce?
- ❏ How can you be more honest in your dealings with others?

Meditate on the titles of God in verses 7–10. How do these descriptions of God motivate you to seek him?

Spend time worshiping God with prayers of confession, petition, thanksgiving, and praise.

6

The Ultimate Vision

REVELATION 21:9–27

When a group convenes for Bible study, they are likely to suggest the book of Revelation. People have always been fascinated by the future, often with curiosity about the timetable of coming events.

But Revelation was not written to provide that information. The final victory of Christ over Satan is painted in broad brush strokes. The book closes with a glorious vision of the Holy City, where the pure in heart will perfectly see God without the distortion of sin. In our final study we will consider the implications of this future promise for present living.

1. When you see or hear the word *heaven*, what comes to your mind?

2. Read Revelation 21:9–27. The angel describes the church as "the bride, the wife of the Lamb" (v. 9). How does this image help you understand our eternal relationship with Jesus Christ?

Do you think of your relationship with Christ in such intimate terms? Why or why not?

3. Surprisingly, when the angel shows John the bride, he doesn't see a woman but rather "the Holy City, Jerusalem" (v. 10). How does a holy city present a different picture of our future life with Christ?

4. John gives an elaborate description of the city in verses 10–21. What overall impression is he trying to make?

5. Like the Most Holy Place of the tabernacle and temple, the Holy City is a perfect cube (v. 16; see also 1 Kings 6:19–20). Why do you think John makes this subtle comparison?

6. In the ancient world, every major city had at least one central temple. In contrast, what do you think John means when he says, "the Lord God Almighty and the Lamb are its temple" (v. 22)?

7. The glory of God will make the sun and moon unnecessary (vv. 23–25). What images come to mind when you think of God's glory (see also Ex. 40:34–35; 1 Kings 8:10–11; Mark 9:2–3, 7)?

8. How do you respond to the idea of living eternally in the midst of God's glory?

9. Who will be excluded from the Holy City, and who will be included (v. 27; see also 21: 6–8; 22:14–15)?

10. Throughout this chapter John stresses that holiness and purity will characterize life in God's kingdom. What incentive does this give you to live a holy and pure life now?

11. In a few minutes of silent prayer, ask God to show you anything unholy or impure in your life that needs to be confessed and given up.

MEMORY VERSE

The city does not need the sun or the moon to shine on it, for the glory of God gives it light, and the Lamb is its lamp.

Revelation 21:23

BETWEEN STUDIES

Now that you have studied part of Revelation 21, read slowly through 21–22 to see the overall picture. Then turn to Romans 8:18–39. There Paul glimpses the ultimate vision of the creation's redemption and then gives strong encouragement to Christians, who have much to endure before that vision becomes reality.

Leader's Notes

Leading a Bible discussion—especially for the first time—can make you feel both nervous and excited. If you are nervous, realize that you are in good company. Many biblical leaders, such as Moses, Joshua, and the apostle Paul, felt nervous and inadequate to lead others (see, for example, 1 Corinthians 2:3). Yet God's grace was sufficient for them, just as it will be for you.

Some excitement is also natural. Your leadership is a gift to the others in the group. Keep in mind, however, that other group members also share responsibility for the group. Your role is simply to stimulate discussion by asking questions and encouraging people to respond. The suggestions listed below can help you to be an effective leader.

PREPARING TO LEAD

1. Ask God to help you understand and apply the passage to your own life. Unless that happens, you will not be prepared to lead others.

2. Carefully work through each question in the study guide. Meditate and reflect on the passage as you formulate your answers.

3. Familiarize yourself with the leader's notes for the study. These will help you understand the purpose of the study and will provide valuable information about the questions in the study.

4. Pray for the various members of the group. Ask God to use these studies to make you better disciples of Jesus Christ.

5. Before the first meeting, make sure each person has a study guide. Encourage them to prepare beforehand for each study.

LEADING THE STUDY

1. Begin the study on time. If people realize that the study begins on schedule, they will work harder to arrive on time.

2. At the beginning of your first time together, explain that these studies are designed to be discussions, not lectures. Encourage everyone to participate, but realize that some may be hesitant to speak during the first few sessions.

3. Read the introductory paragraph at the beginning of the discussion. This will orient the group to the passage being studied.

4. Read the passage aloud. You may choose to do this yourself, or you might ask for volunteers.

5. The questions in the guide are designed to be used just as they are written. If you wish, you may simply read each one aloud to the group. Or you may prefer to express them in your own words. Unnecessary rewording of the questions, however, is not recommended.

6. Don't be afraid of silence. People in the group may need time to think before responding.

7. Avoid answering your own questions. If necessary, rephrase a question until it is clearly understood. Even an eager group will quickly become passive and silent if they think the leader will do most of the talking.

8. Encourage more than one answer to each question. Ask, "What do the rest of you think?" or "Anyone else?" until several people have had a chance to respond.

9. Try to be affirming whenever possible. Let people know you appreciate their insights into the passage.

10. Never reject an answer. If it is clearly wrong, ask, "Which verse led you to that conclusion?" Or let the group handle the problem by asking them what they think about the question.

11. Avoid going off on tangents. If people wander off course, gently bring them back to the passage being considered.

12. Conclude your time together with conversational prayer. Ask God to help you apply those things that you learned in the study.

13. End on time. This will be easier if you control the pace of the discussion by not spending too much time on some questions or too little on others.

Many more suggestions and helps are found in the book *Leading Bible Discussions* (InterVarsity Press). Reading it would be well worth your time.

STUDY 1
Purifying Our Thoughts
MATTHEW 5:21–22, 27–30; 23:23–32

Purpose: To grasp why we need to purify our thoughts in order to have pure actions.

Background Matthew has structured his Gospel in alternating sections of narrative and teaching. The first four chapters report events connected with Jesus' birth; the ministry of John the Baptist; Jesus' baptism, temptation, and initial ministry; and his call of twelve disciples. Chapters 5–7 comprise teachings called the Sermon on the Mount, which begins with the eight Beatitudes.

This study focuses on controversial questions of murder and adultery. We then turn to Jesus' teaching about right living and hypocrisy in a sermon near the end of his earthly life.

Question 1 Every study begins with an "approach question," which is discussed *before* reading the passage. An approach question is designed to do three things.

First, it helps to break the ice. Because an approach question doesn't require any knowledge of the passage or any special preparation, it can get people talking and can help them to warm up to each other.

Second, an approach question can motivate people to study the passage at hand. At the beginning of the study, people in the group aren't necessarily ready to jump into the world of the Bible. Their minds may be on other things (their kids, a problem at work, an upcoming meeting) that have nothing to do with the study. An approach question can capture their interest and draw them into the discussion by raising important issues related to the study. The question becomes a bridge between their personal lives and the answers found in Scripture.

Third, a good approach question can reveal where people's thoughts or feelings need to be transformed by Scripture. That is why it is important to ask the approach question *before* reading the passage. The passage might inhibit the spontaneous, honest answers people might have given, because they feel compelled to give biblical answers. The approach question allows them to compare their personal thoughts and feelings with what they later discover in Scripture.

Question 2 Two main ways of reading a Scripture passage are recommended. 1. Get volunteers to read aloud a paragraph at a time. A common procedure to avoid is reading around the circle one verse at a time, because the members tend to concentrate on their own verse and do not really hear the others. 2. For longer passages, have the group read silently.

"Raca" is an Aramaic term of contempt that may mean "empty-headed." Jesus refers to three levels of conviction: by a local court, by the supreme court at Jerusalem (Sanhedrin), and by God's final judgment. Although it is not clear how the words "angry," "Raca," and "fool" represent increasing offences, the main point is clear: attitudes and words of hatred are as serious as murder.

Question 4 Jesus introduces his teachings in this chapter with the formula: "You have heard that it was said . . . But I tell you." He then contrasts his instruction with a long-held teaching from the past. This contrast appears to make Jesus' teaching contradict that of the Old Testament. So at the outset, Jesus declares, "Do not think that I have come to abolish the Law or the Prophets; I have not come to abolish them but to fulfill them" (Matt. 5:17). In verse 43 Jesus quotes Old Testament teaching about love: "Love your neighbor as yourself" (Lev. 19:18). It was later rabbinic teaching that added "hate your enemy." Jesus' commands remove overlays of tradition from Old Testament teaching. They also go beyond actions and the letter of the law to inner motives and the spirit of the Law and Prophets.

Questions 6–7 Jesus is not teaching self-mutilation, since obviously that would not eliminate evil desires like lust. Rather he instructs us to eliminate sources of temptation. For example, if the eye is causing us to sin, we should not read certain kinds of literature or view X-rated films. The kind of "spiritual surgery" required will depend on each individual situation.

Question 11 The imperative "Fill up, then, the measure of the sin of your forefathers" (v. 32) is a severely ironical command, the final result of cumulative wickedness throughout many generations.

STUDY 2
Whiter Than Snow
PSALM 51

Purpose: To see David's prayer as an effective model of confession and restoration.

Background Sketch very briefly for the group the historical setting for Psalm 51. David was the second king of Israel who reigned around 1000 B.C. He defeated the nation's enemies and strengthened its borders. One evening he summoned the beautiful Bathsheba, whose husband Uriah was away on combat duty, to spend the night with him. Later, when she reported that she was pregnant, David arranged to have Uriah assigned to the battlefront in a way that insured his death. God then sent the prophet Nathan to condemn him for his grievous sins. Unlike the neighboring kings for whom this conduct would be a routine occurrence, David immediately confessed his sin. Later he composed Psalm 51 as his prayer of repentance.

Question 3 "The opening plea, *have mercy,* is the language of one who has no claim to the favour he begs. But *steadfast love* is a covenant word. For all his unworthiness, David knows that he still belongs; cf. the paradox of the prodigal's words, '*Father . . .* I am no more worthy to be called thy son.' Coming closer still, he [David] appeals to God's tender warmth, in the second word for mercy, an emotional term, used in. e.g., Genesis 43:30 when Joseph's 'heart,' or innermost being, yearned for his brother. It is akin to the New Testament's visceral word for 'moved with compassion'" (Derek Kidner, *Psalms 1–72* [Downers Grove, Ill.: InterVarsity Press, 1973], pp. 189–90).

Question 4 No matter how it may injure others, all sin is ultimately against God as a violation of his laws for living.

Question 8 In verse 11 David's prayer, using Hebrew parallelism, has two phrases with the same meaning: He does not want to lose the experience of God's presence given through the Holy Spirit. David recalled his selection as a young man by the prophet Samuel to succeed Saul as king of Israel. "From that day on the Spirit of the Lord came upon David in power" (1 Sam 16:13; see also 2 Sam 23:1–2). This prayer also recalls the rejection of Saul, the first king, following his disobedience: "Now the Spirit of the Lord had departed from Saul, and an evil spirit from the Lord tormented him" (1 Sam 16:14).

As Christians in the New Covenant, we have the Holy Spirit permanently dwelling within us (John 3:5; Rom. 8:9). So we do not have to fear that he will be taken away. Nevertheless, we can "grieve the Holy Spirit of God" through sinful attitudes, words and actions (Eph 4:30–31). We can also "put out the Spirit's fire" by treating prophecies with contempt (1 Thess. 5:19–20).

STUDY 3
Walking in the Light
1 JOHN 1:1–2:11

Purpose: To discover the dangers of walking in darkness and the joys of walking in the light.

Background The apostle John wrote this letter between A.D. 85–95. He was also the author of the Gospel of John and Revelation. The letter was circulated among churches in Asia that were threatened by false teachers who promoted Gnosticism. This early heresy taught that matter is evil and the spirit is entirely good. It denied that God became human in Jesus Christ since he couldn't be contaminated by a physical body. The false teachers also claimed an elite status beyond good and evil; what might be wrong for lesser people was not sin for the "spiritual" person.

Question 2 John's stress on the physical body of the "Word of life" strikes directly at the first Gnostic error.

Question 4 "'If God made man in his own image,' it is said, 'then man has returned the compliment.' That is the root of most of our problems. All sin is in essence an attack upon the character of God. We are not willing to believe that the living God really is as the Scriptures reveal him to us. We have a vested interest in resisting the claims of the 'transcendental interferer,' as C. S. Lewis once called God. The revelation that *God is light* is not a discovery which John has made as a result of his philosophical explorations, but a message he has received. It was heard *from him,* a clear reference to Jesus Christ, last mentioned at the end of verse 3. As always, the apostolic task was to announce to others what they had heard from the Lord" (David Jackman, *The Message of John's Letters* [Downers Grove, Ill.: InterVarsity Press, 1988], pp. 26–27).

Question 6 John meets head-on the Gnostic claim of sinlessness: (1) *I am not a sinner*—a denial of the sinful nature (v. 8); (2) *I have not sinned*—a denial of sinful actions (v. 10). In claiming the first, we deceive ourselves, and we have a false self-image. The second error is prevalent today in the phrases we use to cloak sinful actions. Adultery becomes "having an affair." Theft is "helping myself to the perks." Selfishness is "standing up for my rights." John diagnoses the problem: "The truth is not in us . . . his word has no place in our lives."

Question 11 Jesus himself taught that the Law and Prophets were summed up in the command to love God and one's neighbor (Matt. 22:37–40). The apostle Paul echoed that the entire law was summed up in a single command, "Love your neighbor as yourself" (Gal. 5:14). Yet Jesus did call it a new commandment: "As I have loved you, so you must love one another" (John 13:34). The newness may lie in the fact that, as John states here, "its truth is seen in him and you" (v. 8). That love was perfectly evident in the life of Jesus and now is to be manifested (even though imperfectly) through his power in the lives of his followers. This is what genuine Christianity is all about.

STUDY 4
A Holy Nation
1 PETER 1:13–2:10

Purpose: To understand what it means to be a "holy nation, a people belonging to God."

Background Around A.D. 60 Emperor Nero initiated a program of persecuting the Christians, whom he considered "atheists" because they refused to worship Roman gods. Peter's first letter was probably written from Rome around A.D. 64. He exhorts his readers to holy living and reaffirms their high calling in the face of the suffering they will endure. Peter set an example when a few years later he was martyred—according to tradition, crucified upside down because he felt unworthy to die in the same position as his Lord.

Question 2 The biblical meaning of *hope* is significantly different from its common use today, which implies uncertainty. For example, when we say, "I hope it is sunny for our picnic tomorrow," we mean that there is a good chance it will rain. In the New Testament, however, *hope* is a present certainty of a future event—Christ's return and our full salvation with him.

Question 4 The quotation "Be holy, because I am holy" is from Leviticus 11:44 and is given in the context of commands against using unclean food and water. The command to be holy is repeated in Leviticus 19:2 and 20:7. It means to be set apart from sin and impurity to God.

Question 5 The NIV's translation "stranger" should be "sojourner." The word Peter uses connotes an alien who lives in a place that is not his home. A stranger can settle down permanently in a new country; the sojourner's stay is only temporary.

Question 6 "In the Hellenistic world a slave might be redeemed by a payment made to his master, sometimes through a temple treasury. The Old Testament law provided for the redemption of slaves, and noted the special privilege of a *go'el,* a close relative who could redeem family members or possessions. In the prophecy of Isaiah, God takes the role of the *go'el* of his people. He makes himself 'next of kin' by the ties of his love. He assures his people that the Creator, the Holy One, has bought back his people as his inheritance"

(Edmund Clowney, *The Message of 1 Peter* [Downers Grove, Ill.: InterVarsity Press, 1988], p. 70).

Question 9 Using a standard English dictionary can help you discover the meaning of biblical words. A Bible dictionary may be even more helpful.

STUDY 5
Preparing to See God
PSALM 24

Purpose: To discover from Psalm 24 how we can prepare to see God.

Background In this majestic psalm the King of Glory moves in a procession from the provinces of his realm to the city at the summit. This liturgy may initially have commemorated a ceremony in the enthronement festival of Israel's king. Or it may have celebrated David's escorting the ark of the Lord "with songs and with harps, lyres, tambourines, cymbals and trumpets" to Mount Zion and Jerusalem which he had recently conquered (1 Chron. 13:8). The church has long used this psalm to celebrate Christ's ascension into the heavenly Jerusalem.

Question 3 At the outset the Lord's rule over all the world and its inhabitants is grounded in his being its Creator. The founding of the earth upon the seas is an allusion to Genesis 1:9–10. This prelude to the procession liturgy declares the Lord to be the Creator, Sustainer and Possessor of the whole world and therefore worthy of worship as the "King of Glory."

Question 7 For verse 4 the NIV has the wording "Who does not lift up his soul to an idol or swear by what is false." The RSV has "Who does not lift up his soul to what is false, and does not swear deceitfully." Both convey the same concept: who does not worship a false god or give false testimony.

Question 9 "This stirring challenge and response (which may have been ritually enacted at the arrival of David's procession at the gates) brings before us in the fewest of words the towering stature of the unseen King, the age-old fortress He is entering to make His own . . . and the link between this climax and the earlier history of

46

redemption—for the expression *mighty in battle* is but a stronger form of God's title of 'warrior' first heard in the song of victory at the Red Sea (Ex. 15:3). The ascent completes a march begun in Egypt . . . If the earth is His (1, 2) and He is holy (3–6), the challenge to the 'ancient doors' is not an exercise in pageantry, but (as in 2 Cor 10:3–5) a battle-cry for the church" (Kidner, *Psalms 1–72*, p. 115).

STUDY 6
The Ultimate Vision
REVELATION 21:9–27

Purpose: To see a vision of the Holy City and how that hope should motivate us to live pure lives now.

Background Early tradition holds that Revelation was written by the apostle John in the latter part of Domitian's reign during A.D. 81–96. However that may be, the "John" of Revelation makes the apostolic claim that the real author is Jesus Christ (Rev. 1:1–2). The book was sent to seven cities of Asia Minor as a circular letter to be read aloud in their meetings. It met real needs of first-century Christians, encouraged them in their persecution, and challenged them to fight the forces of evil.

Question 3 It is important to realize that John is describing the church, the bride of Christ, not a literal city. Michael Wilcock writes: "Christian readers must remind themselves that the bride, the city, is none other than the church of Christ. The churches of John's day, the churches of our own day, all of us are looking into a mirror in these verses. We are not merely spectators—we are ourselves the spectacle: it is we who are 'God's building' (1 Cor. 3:9). The city shown to us here is what we shall be in the age to come, what in a sense we already are, on the level of 'the heavenlies,' and what in our earthly experience God is presently making of us" (*The Message of Revelation* [Downers Grove, Ill.: InterVarsity Press, 1975], p. 207).

Question 4 Robert H. Mounce comments that "the overall picture is of a city of brilliant gold surrounded by a wall inlaid with jasper and resting upon twelve foundations adorned with precious gems of every color and hue. The city is magnificent beyond description. As the eternal dwelling place of God and his people, it is described in language which continually attempts to break free from its own limitations in order to do justice to the reality it so imperfectly describes" (*The Book of Revelation,* The New International Commentary on the New Testament [Grand Rapids, Mich.: Eerdmans, 1977], p. 383).

Question 5 For those familiar with the Old Testament, John's description of the city would bring to mind the Most Holy Place, also known as the Holy of Holies, the earthly dwelling place of God. The shape of the city symbolizes that God has come to dwell among us, as Revelation 21:3 states: "And I heard a loud voice from the throne saying, 'Now the dwelling of God is with man, and he will live with them. They will be his people, and God himself will be with them and be their God."

Question 6 "John turns from this beautiful description of the city to the life within it. In antiquity every notable city had at least one central temple. The New Jerusalem not only differs in this respect from ancient cities but also from all Jewish speculation about the age to come. Illuminated by the overflowing radiance of the presence of the glory of God, the Holy City no longer needs a temple (*naos*). Yet paradoxically it has a temple, for the Lord God Almighty and the Lamb are its temple (v. 22). And in another sense, the whole city is a temple, since it is patterned after the Most Holy Place (v. 16). Jewish expectation was centered on a rebuilt temple and the restoration of the ark of the covenant. In his glorious vision, John sees the fulfillment of these hopes in the total presence of God with his purified people, while the Lamb, the sign of the new covenant, is the fulfillment of the restoration of the ark of the covenant" (Alan F. Johnson, *Revelation*, The Expositor's Bible Commentary, vol. 12, ed. Frank E. Gaebelein [Grand Rapids, Mich.: Zondervan, 1981], p. 597).

Question 9 John makes it clear that "those whose names are written in the Lamb's book of life" are able to enter the Holy City not because of any merit of their own but only because they "washed their robes" in Christ's blood (22:14) and "drink without cost from the spring of the water of life" (21:6).

Yet John clearly states that such people have renounced their former way of life and do not practice the things committed by those excluded from the Holy City: "'Fine linen, bright and clean, was given her to wear.' (Fine linen stands for the righteous acts of the saints.)" (19:8). Those clothed in the righteousness of Christ also adorn themselves with their own righteous acts.